SHERLOCK HOUNDS

Our heroic search and rescue dogs

Written by Phyllis J. Perry

Thanks to the following for their help and cooperation
in the preparation of this material:

Maria Neary, Front Range Rescue Dogs, in Boulder, Colorado,

and the National Association for Search and Rescue
in Fairfax, Virginia

—P.J.P.

Text copyright © 2006 by Phyllis J. Perry
Photographs copyright: Cover (left), back cover, p. 1: © Andrea Booher/FEMA News Photo;
cover (center): © Anita Westervelt/FEMA News Photo; cover (right): © Roberta Casaliggi;
p. 4: © David Freund; p. 5: © Focus Group/Alamy; p. 6: © Vedros & Associates/The Image Bank/Getty
Images, Inc.; p. 7: © Royalty-Free/CORBIS; p. 9: © Preston Keres/U.S. Navy; p. 10: © Steven K. Doi/
ZUMA/CORBIS; p. 11: © Jan Ingebrigtsen; pp. 14, 20, 25, 29: © Cliff A. Weaver; p. 15: © Tom Nebbia/
CORBIS; pp. 16, 21: © Owen Franken/CORBIS; p. 18: © Dale C. Spartas/CORBIS; p. 19: © David Such; p.
22: Courtesy of WOLVES and International Procurement Services (Overseas) Ltd.; p. 23: © SHOUT/Alamy;
p. 26: © Jean-Bernard Vernier/CORBIS SYGMA; p. 27: © William Stevenson/Alamy; p. 30:
© Frank Naylor/Alamy

For information contact:

MONDO Publishing
980 Avenue of the Americas
New York, NY 10018

Visit our website www.mondopub.com

Printed in China

09 10 11 12   9 8 7 6 5 4 3 2

ISBN 1-59336-728-7 (PB)

Designed by Witz End Design

Library of Congress Cataloging-in-Publication Data

Perry, Phyllis Jean.
  Sherlock hounds : our heroic search and rescue dogs / by Phyllis J. Perry.
     p. cm.
  Includes index.
  ISBN 1-59336-728-7 (pbk.)
  1. Search dogs--Juvenile literature. 2. Rescue dogs--Juvenile literature.
  3. Search and rescue operations--Juvenile literature. I. Title.
SF428.73.P47 2006
636.73--dc22

                    2005022662

Contents

Lost in the Woods

Imagine that you are out hiking in the woods. It's a beautiful day and you're feeling great, enjoying the breeze rustling through the pine trees. You breathe in the fresh, sweet-smelling air and listen to the birds chirping and the sound of pine needles scrunching under your feet.

It happens gradually as you're hiking and taking in all that beauty. Slowly an awful feeling grows in the pit of your stomach. Suddenly you don't recognize anything in sight. You realize it's been ages since you saw another hiker. Then it hits you: you're lost! You try to keep calm, but you feel the panic rising.

Where is everyone? Which way leads back to camp? Will anyone find you? Should you stay put or keep walking? What if you have to spend the night in the woods alone? Are there any wild animals around? Do you have any food in your backpack?

Usually this moment of panic passes. With a flood of relief, you see another hiker up ahead, or else you recognize a familiar landmark, and the way back to camp becomes clear to you. Slowly your heart stops pounding, and that funny feeling in your stomach disappears. Before long you're back with family and friends enjoying the day. You may even feel a little foolish for having felt so afraid, and you might not mention your moment of panic to anyone.

But what if you were really lost? What then? Depending on where you live, it's entirely possible that instead of a human, a dog would be the first one to come to your rescue. This wouldn't be an ordinary dog

stumbling upon you by accident while out chasing squirrels; it would be a dog as trained in sleuthing and detecting as old Sherlock Holmes himself. This "Sherlock Hound" would be a trained search and rescue dog—part of a **SAR (Search and Rescue) Team** that includes the dog and its human handler.

If you *were* lost, you'd be lucky to have a Search and Rescue Team trying to find you. Helicopters have a 20 percent chance of finding a lost person, and ground searchers have a 15 percent chance. But search dog teams are rated as having a 70 percent success rate when looking for a missing person.

Chapter 1

About Search and Rescue Dog Units

Search and Rescue Teams have been used for hundreds of years in other countries to locate missing persons. The first search and rescue dogs were Saint Bernards in Switzerland. They lived with religious monks in the Great Saint Bernard Mountain Pass in the Alps. These monks looked for lost travelers, relying on their dogs' hardiness, determination, and, most importantly, keen sense of smell to help them. It is estimated that Saint Bernards rescued 2,000 people during the eighteenth and nineteenth centuries.

However, it has only been in the past few years that dogs have become common in search and rescue **missions** in the United States. The first organization dedicated to training search and rescue dogs was the American Rescue Dog Association, which was founded in 1972 by Bill and Jean Syrotuck. The idea caught on quickly, and there are now over 150 search

Saint Bernard with a cask around neck in the snow

and rescue teams in North America. These volunteer organizations, called **SAR (Search and Rescue) Units**, are made up of support personnel as well as trained Search and Rescue Teams.

SAR Units are most common in states where there are mountains, national parks, and wilderness and recreation areas that attract campers, climbers, hikers, and skiers. But there are some cities and counties, such as Santa Barbara County in California, that have urban SAR Teams. More than 30 states have at least one Search and Rescue Unit. The main office of the National Association for Search and Rescue (NASAR)—the organization that oversees all the local state SAR Units—is located in Fairfax, Virginia, outside of Washington, D.C.

SAR handler and dog

There is also a United States International Search and Rescue Team, which is called upon to assist in disasters around the world. The team works under the direction of the U.S. Office of Foreign Disaster Assistance. This international team is made up of about 30 members, and only the best local dogs and handlers are asked to be a part of it. In addition to the dogs and their handlers, the team also includes support members, such as engineers, firefighters, and doctors.

A dog's incredible sense of smell isn't the only resource a SAR Unit has. Units also use high-tech equipment during their people-finding missions. In some cases, searchers may lower a long electronic cable containing tiny listening devices through piles of wreckage and **debris** in an attempt to detect heartbeats and breathing. They may also lower tiny cameras through rubble to look for human shapes and movements, and they use other instruments to detect body heat.

Basic Types of Searches

There are several different types of search missions that Search and Rescue Units undertake, including wilderness, water, evidence, and disaster. In a wilderness search (also called an area search), dogs look for people lost in woods, mountains, and even caves. A single trained search dog is able to do the work of approximately a dozen human searchers, covering a square mile (2.6 sq km) in two hours. A water search begins when it's suspected that someone has drowned. Evidence searches involve different kinds of police work, usually connected with a crime. For example, if a person is found murdered and the killer has left behind some evidence—a piece of clothing or another personal item—the dog will follow the killer's scent and help the police find him or her. Disaster searches take place after hurricanes, floods, fires, train wrecks, earthquakes, bombings, explosions, and **avalanches**.

These dramatic searches often make newspaper headlines or television news. For example, international SAR Units made world news in 1988 after they helped rescue survivors of an earthquake in Armenia. And in 1987, Fran Lieser and her dog Pockets were front-page news when they helped find a toddler lost in the Rocky Mountains of Colorado. In Ohio one particular dog frequently makes the news. Parker, a 168-pound (76.3-kg) black Newfoundland that works with a **paramedic**, has participated in more than 40 water searches for drowning victims.

On April 19, 1995, the worst terrorist bombing to occur in the United States took place in Oklahoma City, when the Alfred P. Murrah Federal Building was destroyed, killing 168 people. Search and rescue dogs were on the scene to assist in locating victims.

That disaster paled in comparison to the one that occurred on September 11, 2001. When terrorists crashed planes into the World Trade Center in New York City, thousands of people were killed or injured. In addition to the many police, firefighters, and paramedics who participated in the rescue mission,

"Disaster Dogs," as they were called, also did their part. Many of these dogs worked 12-hour shifts in the rubble with their handlers. While the human searchers wore respirator masks to protect themselves from the thick dust and smoke, the dogs, who had to rely on their noses, could not.

A rescue dog is transported out of the World Trade Center debris, September 2001.

A natural disaster that Search and Rescue Teams from many parts of the world responded to was the Indian Ocean tsunami in December 2004. Teams searched through the destruction and rubble for survivors and also helped recover bodies of those who had died.

Signals

Search and rescue dogs alert, or signal, their discoveries in many ways. One dog may bark, while another stops still and pricks up its ears. Water rescue dogs signal their handlers when they have caught the scent of a person underwater. One water rescue dog may lean over the edge of the boat and bite at the water, while another may signal by barking, whining, or circling the boat. A typical alert for an avalanche rescue dog is to start digging above where the victim is buried.

SAR Teams are used often by forest rangers and sheriffs' departments to assist in foot searches for lost persons. The teams may help find children who have become lost in the wilderness or those who have gone missing in urban areas. The SAR Units may also help search for elderly people who have become confused and wandered away from nursing homes or hospitals.

Occasionally the search for a lost person leads to the recovery of a murder victim. Then SAR Teams specializing in criminal searches and crime scene work are called in. A dog's excellent sense of smell can help the team pick up and follow the suspected murderer's trail. An officer often accompanies a SAR Team in case the criminal is found and an arrest needs to be made.

Police dog with law enforcement officer

Makeup of Search and Rescue Units

Most Search and Rescue Units—including the dogs, handlers, and other support personnel—are volunteers. Those involved must have employers and family members who understand that they may have to drop everything at a moment's notice to participate in a search and rescue operation. After all, someone's life may depend on the team's quick response. Well over half of all the search and rescue volunteers in the United States are female.

These volunteers do not earn a salary for helping to locate missing persons or disaster and accident victims. They may, however, accept donations to the organization they represent. For example, a corporation may pay for airfares, help cover the cost of training the volunteers, or donate equipment to a Search and Rescue Team. Some SAR Units actively fundraise so they are able to purchase equipment they need, such as radios and telephone pagers, or so they can pay for the training of their members.

The Front Range Rescue Dogs (FRRD), with headquarters in Boulder, Colorado, is a typical SAR Unit. Active since 1984, its motto is "People and Dogs Committed to Serving Our Community." The unit is made up of about 32 human volunteers and 15 dogs, and they are involved in 35 to 40 searches a year.

The volunteers in Front Range Rescue Dogs have varied backgrounds, including teaching, nursing, homemaking, and business, and the dogs are of many different breeds. The handlers and dogs need to spend a lot of time together in order to become a good team. Maria Neary, an FRRD member whose canine partner is her golden retriever, Emma, says, "Search and rescue training isn't easy for dogs or humans. Sometimes in your early training, you ask, 'Will my dog make it?'" Maria admits that sometimes you even wonder, "Will I make it?"

Colorado Front Range Rescue dog with handler

Chapter 2

What Makes a Dog a Search and Rescue Dog?

You've learned about the types of people who are likely to become involved as Search and Rescue Team volunteers. But what about the dogs that join these important, life-saving units? You've read that they can be different breeds, but what characteristics and abilities must these dogs have to be successful search and rescue animals?

Tests That SAR Dogs Must Pass

A dog training to be part of a SAR Unit must learn many different tasks. Dog handler Maria Neary says that each step of the training is a challenge for both dog and handler, and she admits, "Sometimes I make mistakes. But my dog, Emma, forgives me when I do, and she is able to quickly relearn the right way even if I've done something wrong the first time. Dogs need to be corrected, but most of all, they need praise, rewards, and affection."

In order to become a fully trained search and rescue dog, the animal must pass four tests. Often the first test is locating a person at night in an area measuring a half-mile by a half-mile (.8 x .8 km). The second test is finding a person during the day in a one-square-mile (2.6-sq-km) area. The next test involves finding multiple people. And the final test is finding three out of five items—which have been scattered around a half-mile by half-mile area—belonging to a person pretending to be the victim.

When doing an item search, it is best if the dog is trained to just sit still next to the item after finding it and then bark to alert its handler of the discovery. This way, other clues that might be in the area and that might help in locating the missing person won't be disturbed. Unfortunately some dogs become so excited about finding what they've been looking for that they pick up the item in their mouth and return it to their handler.

Choosing the Right Dog

Many types of dogs are used in search and rescue missions. However, there is disagreement over which breeds are the most successful. Some SAR Units use a variety of breeds, including mixed breeds, while others prefer just one particular breed. Many experts believe success in search and rescue is due more to the individual dog than to its breed.

The U.S. International Search and Rescue Team has included the following breeds: Labrador retriever, giant schnauzer, golden retriever, rottweiler, Doberman pinscher, Australian cattle dog, and Newfoundland. Search and Rescue Dogs of Colorado (SARDOC) has used Australian shepherds, German shepherds, Labrador retrievers, Chesapeake Bay retrievers, golden retrievers, bloodhounds, border collies, and terrier mixes as its search and rescue dogs.

 ## Smelly Sneakers Are Easy to Trace!

Some of a victim's or missing person's personal items hold a scent better than others. For example, a set of keys will not keep its owner's scent as well as a wallet. Damp clothes keep a scent longer than clothes left in a hot, dusty spot. Shoes hold a scent better than most other personal items.

The Newfoundland, which was originally bred on the island of Newfoundland in Canada, is a favorite of many handlers. This breed learns quickly and seems to have natural lifesaving instincts. The Newfoundland, often called a "Newfie" or "Newf" for short, is as much at home in water as on dry land.

Because it takes so much time and effort to train a SAR dog, it is important that the right dogs are chosen from the beginning. In selecting a dog, several things must be considered. Is the dog friendly toward people? Is it easily distracted by other dogs or animals? Does the dog do a lot of unnecessary barking? Is it frightened by traffic or loud noises? Does it get carsick? Is it in excellent physical condition? Is the dog "sniffy"—that is, inclined toward using its nose to investigate?

Even if the answers to these questions suggest a particular dog might be a good candidate for a SAR Team, there may be other problems. For example, a dog that's full grown and not a puppy might be too attached to the person who raised it to work well with a new handler. Some experts believe that the best search and rescue dogs are medium-sized—standing 20 to 28 inches (51 to 72 cm) at the shoulder. Both male and female dogs can be successful at search and rescue, but they must be in good health, not overweight or undernourished, and their joints must be disease-free.

SAR dogs can be many different breeds.

Dogs with a double coat of fur—a soft undercoat covered by a stiff, protective topcoat—are able to stay warm enough to search in all kinds of weather. Dogs with curly coats or long fur on their stomachs and legs have trouble in sticky snow and in thick underbrush. Dogs with short coats need to be protected from the weather when they are out in extreme cold.

Since all breeds are expected to cover 3 to 4 miles (4.8 to 6.4 km) for every mile (1.6 km) a person can cover, a search and rescue dog must be strong and agile. The dog must be courageous, have a good temperament, and get along with people and other dogs. The dog must be willing and able to follow directions and not be inclined to run off and chase other animals.

Newfoundlands

Newfoundlands are champion water rescuers. These large dogs, which can weigh 150 pounds (68 kg), dive and swim underwater easily. Newfoundlands do not "dog paddle," but rather swim with strong strokes. A dense, oily coat keeps the dog warm and repels water. Its ears lie close to the body, which helps keep water out, and its strong, muscled tail helps the dog turn and move in the water.

Newfoundlands training for water rescue

However, the most important quality in a really successful Sherlock Hound is a good nose. A dog's sense of smell is much better than a human's. Humans have about 5 million **olfactory** cells (cells used for smelling), while large dogs, such as German shepherds, have an estimated 220 million scent cells. And a dog's scent cells are spread over a much larger area than a human's, which enables the dog to pick up more subtle scents. Dogs with long noses and wide nostrils are the most efficient smellers.

Bloodhounds, which are preferred by many handlers for ground tracking, have a keen sense of smell that is unequaled. The bloodhound's floppy ears help channel the scent particles toward the nose. Loose and droopy skin over its eyes protects it from weeds and brush, while loose skin over its entire face traps scents in the folds.

Rescue efforts during the 1985 Mexico City earthquake

A search and rescue dog's keen sense of smell is so important that dogs being flown to disaster areas are sometimes treated differently from ordinary airplane **cargo**. For example, on a flight to Mexico, where a dog named Aly and his handler Caroline Hebard, a member of the U.S. International Search and Rescue Team, were going to help in a disaster, Aly got to ride in the passenger section of the airplane instead of the cargo hold. If the dog had been left waiting outside the plane like other cargo while the plane was being loaded and unloaded, fumes from the jet engines could have ruined his sense of smell for over 24 hours. This would have prevented him from doing his job. During one rescue mission in Mexico City in 1985, Aly searched through the ruins of Juarez Hospital after a massive earthquake. The dog found five doctors still alive in the rubble.

Chapter 3

Training SAR Teams

As you might imagine, a lot of time and effort goes into becoming a qualified member of a Search and Rescue Team. It's hard work for everyone involved, including the handlers and the dogs. Not everyone (or every dog!) has what it takes.

Training the Search and Rescue Dog

Both time and patience are required to train a search and rescue dog. In order for a dog and handler to become an operational SAR Team, about 18 months to two years of training is needed. During the first year of training, there are usually three to five sessions a week. Dogs learn such voice commands as "Find!," "Search!," and "Bring!" They also learn to follow hand signals.

Many teams-in-training work under the supervision of other search and rescue experts. These experienced trainers observe the new team working and offer valuable advice and assistance that improve results and cut down on a new team's training time. Just as students learn the "Three R's"—reading, 'riting, and 'rithmetic—in school, dogs in search and rescue school have their own "Three R's," which are the basic skills they must learn in their training: relate, repeat, reward.

First, the trainers set up a typical search and rescue challenge. By handling the dog a certain way during the exercise, they can train the dog to *relate* its actions to the challenge. For example, the dog may be commanded to use its sense of smell to find someone hiding beneath a pile of rubble in a simulation of a disaster rescue. By *repeating* consistent commands such as "Search!" and "Find!," the trainer teaches the dog what it's being asked to do. Finally, the trainer *rewards* the dog's successes and willingness to follow orders with praise and petting.

Some search and rescue training can start when the dog is just a puppy. Puppies want to be with their owners as much as possible, so if their owners hide, puppies will hunt for them. If owners are careful to keep out of sight and conceal the direction in which they have gone, the dog learns to search using its senses of smell and hearing. The more the puppy practices, the better it gets. And searching for its owner is such fun for a puppy that it will do it over and over again. By hiding increasingly farther away from the puppy, the owner helps it get better and better at searching.

Chesapeake Bay retriever puppy in training

Mature dogs can also be trained for search and rescue teams as long as they have been well treated by previous owners. A dog that's been mistreated usually cannot develop the trust in its human handler that's essential to learning the skills needed to be a search and rescue dog.

Dogs in training are usually first certified for wilderness or area searches. Dogs on such missions often wear a harness and an orange vest, called a **shabrack**, with either the word "Rescue" or a cross printed on it. This is helpful because the person who is the subject of the search might be hurt and is usually frightened. Seeing a dog in a shabrack reassures the person that this isn't a wild or dangerous dog.

SAR dog wearing a shabrack

Wilderness search dogs are sometimes trained not to bark upon locating a missing person, because this can further frighten a hurt and scared victim. Instead, dogs are trained to signal their discovery in some other way. Each dog has its own signal; some prick up their ears when they first sight the victim, while others wag their tails. One trained SAR dog would bring a stick to its handler to signal that it had made a discovery. This dog enjoyed playing fetch with its owner, and bringing a stick to its handler was the dog's way of saying that it had finished its work and it was now time to play. Each team has its own rewards.

Finding places to practice search and rescue can be a challenge for SAR Teams. Teams can't keep using the same areas, because the dogs will get used to them. Also each practice area must be large enough so that there's space for several dogs to work without getting in each other's way.

Once initial training is complete, some SAR Teams go on to specialize in disaster debris searches, avalanche rescue, or water rescue. Depending on the breed, a trained SAR dog usually works either until it is about 10 years old or is past its peak physical condition. By that time its handler needs to have another dog trained and ready to take over.

Harness Lift

When a search mission is to take place in an area that's hard to access on foot, a search and rescue dog may be fitted with a harness, clipped to a towrope, and lifted and carried by helicopter into the remote area.

Dog being trained for harness work

Training the Human Half of the Team

The dog is only one part of the SAR Team. People who volunteer to be SAR dog handlers know they are signing up to be on call 24 hours a day, 365 days a year. It can be physically challenging and grueling work. Volunteers are also aware that they will need to complete a difficult training course. These dog-handlers-in-training must become qualified in such areas as first aid, using a compass, and using a radio transmitter. Along with other support members in a SAR Unit, they must attend training sessions to learn how to handle **hazardous** materials and what to do at a disaster scene. They may even practice avalanche rescue.

Many dog handlers carry beepers and cellphones with them at all times. This way they can be reached quickly in case their help is needed. Handlers also often keep a bag packed with search and rescue supplies, such as food, water, a flashlight, gloves, and a compass, so they will be ready to go at a moment's notice. In many cases, a quick response time is the difference between a victim's surviving or not. Search and rescue volunteers know that they may be asked to pick up and leave their jobs and homes quickly to respond to a request for search and rescue help.

When a SAR Team is on a disaster rescue mission, handlers often dress in orange coveralls so they can be seen easily. They wear boots and gloves to protect themselves from sharp objects in the debris, and in some circumstances, they wear a miner's hat with a light on it so they can see inside dark rubble. A SAR Team is usually equipped to work at a disaster site for three to five days, which means bringing along supplies, such as a sleeping bag, tent, water purifier, portable stove, portable radio, hard hat, gloves, boots, flashlight, compass, thermos, food, and medical supplies.

Human SAR workers wearing easily spotted orange coveralls

How Do Dogs Locate People?

Every human being gives off a different scent. These unique scents are what search and rescue dogs learn to pick up and track on their missions. Humans continually shed **microscopic particles** called **scurf**, and it's these particles that carry their individual scent. Scurf is made up of sweat, pieces of hair, and tiny dead skin cells. Even while standing still, your body sheds and replaces about 50 million dead skin and hair cells a day. Scurf can be carried by the wind or deposited on plants or other surfaces. Therefore the scent that a SAR dog uses to find a missing person is affected by winds, rain, snow, and temperature. The dog's handler must be aware of how these factors will affect the search.

Most trainers begin by teaching a dog the **air scenting** method. In air scenting, the dog sniffs the air and follows any human scent it picks up. The dog continues to follow the scent until the person is discovered. This method is most commonly used to find lost hikers and children who wander away. It is also particularly useful at night and in dense brush—conditions in which human searchers aren't able to see much.

Although having an excellent nose is crucial, a search and rescue dog also uses its other senses during missions. It listens carefully for movement to detect the direction in which a missing person is moving. It uses its eyesight, which is quite good even at night, to help locate the person. The dog also uses its paws to dig at debris and uncover a trapped person.

Once the dog has mastered air scent search, other training options are possible. Agile dogs that help with disaster rescues are trained to find human scents that drift up out of piles of debris from buildings knocked down by earthquakes, bombs, and so on. In avalanche rescue, the dog is trained to pick up human scents coming up to the surface through many feet of snow.

 ## WOLVES

When a missing person is trapped in a space that's too small for an adult to enter, a search and rescue dog will often be outfitted with a Wireless Operationally Linked Electronic and Video Exploration System (WOLVES). The equipment, worn by the dog, consists of tiny cameras, microphones, and receivers that relay images back to the rescuers and allow them to speak to the missing person as well. This helps rescuers know what assistance might be necessary to save the victim.

Chapter 4

Types of Search and Rescue

There are four main types of search and rescue missions, and each type has its own specially trained and qualified SAR Units and Teams. A team that's been trained to do Area Search and Rescue, for example, won't go out on avalanche missions, just as Water Search and Rescue Teams won't be sent on debris missions.

Area Search and Rescue

The most common type of search and rescue mission using dogs is probably a wilderness, or area, rescue. The first step is for the dog and its handler to be brought to the missing person's Place Last Seen (PLS). This could be a campsite or a hiking trail. There, they begin their search. In addition to air scenting, which enables a dog to pick up the general

A bloodhound smells an article of clothing belonging to a missing person.

scent of a human, most dogs are trained to track as well. A **tracking** dog may be given an article of clothing from the missing person and pick up the specific person's scent that way.

A particular area search and rescue dog may specialize in either air scenting or ground tracking, while another dog might be trained in both. At the start of a search, dogs may wear special vests to identify them, but they are not on leashes. The SAR dog will lift its head to sniff the wind and may also sniff the ground and low-growing plants to locate the missing person's scent. Once a dog has found a scent and begins to track or trail the missing person, it is usually outfitted with a chest harness or leash. Search and rescue dogs learn to ignore all other distractions while they follow one particular scent.

On one mission, searcher Sandy Bryson and her dog Hobo responded to a request from the National Park Service rangers—a seven-year-old boy had gone missing overnight from a campground in Yosemite National Park in California. Hobo tracked the boy down about a mile and a half (2.4 km) from camp.

Another time, Sandy Bryson and her other dog, Thunder, assisted the Butte County Sheriff's Department in California in locating a two-year-old girl who had wandered off and was lost in the foothills of the Sierra Nevada Mountains. Thunder found the girl almost 4 miles (6.4 km) from the point where she'd been last seen.

In both of these cases, the lost child was found quite a distance from the Place Last Seen. Many SAR Unit members visit schools and scout groups to give kids information about what to do if they ever get lost. One of the most important instructions they give is to stay in one place and not wander around. It's easier for the dog and its handler to follow the trail of a person who stays put.

Under good conditions a dog can follow a trail that is up to 48 hours old. Although all handlers do not agree about how SAR dogs should be trained, most handlers train their dogs in air scenting first, in tracking next, and finally in other specialized search methods.

Debris Search and Rescue

When a major disaster—fire, flood, earthquake, tornado, explosion—occurs in a populated area, SAR Units are often called in to search the wreckage for survivors. Often in disasters, buildings are destroyed, and in some cases they collapse, trapping people under the debris. The dogs don't wear shabracks in debris search and rescue because the orange vests could catch on broken concrete and bits of wood, preventing them from doing their job.

A SAR dog sniffs around and searches through debris after a house fire.

As in most search and rescue attempts, time is crucial in a debris search. The people caught beneath the rubble could be badly injured. Even if they're not hurt, there's a good chance they are without food and water. There could be very little air to breathe, and the temperature under the rubble could be dangerously high. Locating victims quickly can make the difference between finding a person alive or dead.

In cases where there's been a building fire or explosion, a search and rescue dog's handler or a firefighter may carry the dog over broken glass and hot surfaces to protect the animal's feet. However, some search and rescue dogs wear sturdy booties on their feet for protection. Debris search and rescue is challenging, because during the search process, there's always a risk that rescuers—dogs or people—will loosen broken timbers and rocks that could then fall and further injure someone. During training to be a part of a debris SAR Team, trainees learn how to prevent this kind of accident.

Avalanche Search and Rescue

A mountain's deep snow and steep slopes attract many daring skiers, but sometimes large blocks of snow break off and crash downhill, forming an avalanche. An avalanche can reach a speed of almost 200 miles (320 km) per hour. It is estimated that in the mountains of the western United States, 100,000 avalanches occur each year. Sometimes skiers or hikers are buried in one of these avalanches. Search and rescue dogs are brought in to help locate them.

On the night of February 4, 1989, a terrible storm raged on Wolf Creek Pass in Colorado. It was just after ten o'clock at night when Mark Moore, a snowplow driver for the Colorado Department of Transportation, stopped his plow to adjust the blade angle. Suddenly an avalanche came roaring down and struck him. He was thrown to the side of the road and buried.

A SAR dog sniffs the snow and tries to find survivors after an avalanche.

Almost an hour passed before anyone noticed he was missing. Then finally the call for rescuers went out. Susan Lester and her dog, Avy, were contacted; they arrived at the scene of the avalanche at 12:35 A.M. Luckily the avalanche hadn't buried the snowplow, so Avy was put in the vehicle's driver's seat to get Mark Moore's scent. Within minutes, Avy had sniffed out the buried man. Shovelers dug down 5 feet (1.5 m) and uncovered Mark.

Mark Moore survived even though he had been buried for three hours. This is highly unusual. Luckily Mark was holding one of his hands in front of his face when the avalanche buried him. This enabled him to carve out a space in the snow around his face, which gave him some breathing room.

In Austria, France, and Switzerland, avalanche rescue dogs have been used successfully since the end of World War II. Hundreds of lives have been saved by these dogs. The way most avalanche rescue dogs alert their team that they've located a body is by digging at the spot where the person is buried.

Getting Up a Mountain

During a search and rescue mission after an avalanche, it is sometimes necessary for the handler and dog to ride a chairlift up a mountain. A good avalanche search and rescue dog must willingly climb onto the chairlift and ride calmly to the top.

In the United States, however, dogs weren't regularly used in avalanche search and rescue until the 1980s. The first live rescue by avalanche dogs in the United States was made in 1982, in California's Sierra Nevada Mountains. A search and rescue team called WOOF (Wilderness Finders, Inc.), which included a German shepherd named Bridget, was called in. By the time the team arrived, a woman named Anna Conrad had been buried in a demolished building under more than 10 feet (3 m) of snow for five days. Bridget found her alive, and they both made history. Bridget even made a trip to the hospital to visit Anna as she recovered.

The only problem with using dogs in avalanche rescue is the time it takes to get them to the scene. Few ski areas in the United States have trained dogs nearby. Therefore a victim may suffocate before the dog arrives and begins the search. However a recent invention imitates the ability of avalanche search and rescue dogs. This rescue device, which is currently in limited use in Europe, is a probe that senses carbon dioxide levels. (Humans exhale carbon dioxide when they breathe.) When inserted into the snow, the probe can "sniff out" the location of a buried victim. This mechanical avalanche dog, called a "snuffler," hasn't yet been used enough to determine just how helpful it is.

Water Search and Rescue

Search and rescue dogs are also used to find drowning victims. Certain breeds, such as Labradors and golden retrievers, which take well to water, and German shepherds, which are strong swimmers, are well-suited to this type of rescue. Some dogs, however, don't like the water and become nervous in boats.

As in avalanche search and rescue, water search victims rarely turn up alive. The job of water search and rescue dogs is to help find the bodies of people who are missing, searching in nearby ponds, lakes, and rivers. A water rescue dog is trained either to ride in the front of the search boat, to swim out to the search area, or sometimes to work from the shoreline.

These dogs are able to pick up a person's scent bubbling up through the water. When that happens, the usual alert from a dog in a boat may be whining, circling, or running from front to back as the boat passes over the spot where the body is. In murky water this alert from the dog can save the local police from having to search the entire body of water, which might take days. Once a body is found, the family of the victim can stop wondering what happened, and local officials can stop the time-consuming and expensive search for the missing person. It is a sad but important duty.

To train a dog in water search and rescue, a diver wearing scuba gear goes underwater and pretends to be a drowned person by lingering at a spot a few feet below the surface. The dog either swims out or is taken out on a boat, and it learns to search for the diver by trying to pick up his or her scent. When a dog working from the shore has found a scent, it alerts its handler by barking and may start to swim out to the victim. The first training dives are made in shallow water; if there is a breeze, scents are carried well. The training gets gradually more difficult as the diver moves to deeper water farther from shore. In some training sessions, divers have gone as far as 30 feet (9.1 m) below the surface and have been located by the dog-in-training.

Training a dog in water search and rescue

For SAR Teams training in water rescue, it is important to consider the safety of both dogs and the divers. Teams must keep a lookout for boats with propellers, which can be dangerous to dogs and swimmers. The dogs also need breaks to dry out and rest.

Other Jobs For Dogs

Since the United States began using dogs in search and rescue missions, the need, number, and diversity of teams has greatly increased. The National Association for Search and Rescue estimates that 50,000 search and rescue missions are undertaken each year in the United States. Many of these include canine SAR Units—and the number increases every year.

Being involved in search and rescue is only one of the many ways dogs help people. Some are guide dogs that assist the blind, while others help those who are hearing-impaired. Dogs are used at airports to sniff out drugs and explosives that criminals might be trying to smuggle into the country. Dogs travel in police cars and help patrol city neighborhoods. They help firefighters, too. Some dogs learn to pick up the scent of gasoline, kerosene, or paint thinner—products that can be used to start a fire.

There's no doubt that the jobs that dogs do are extremely important. Just ask a person who has been found after being lost for days in the wilderness, or the person who, trapped beneath the rubble of a building after an earthquake, is finally located by a search and rescue dog. These people will tell you that when lost, trapped, or buried alive, no sight is more welcome than a trained search and rescue dog. Sherlock Hounds play a vital role in saving lives and will continue to do so for years to come.

A guide dog helps a blind man get around town.

Glossary

air scenting
When a search and rescue dog sniffs the air to pick up a missing person's scent

avalanche
Large mass of snow, ice, earth, or rocks that comes down a mountainside

debris
Rubbish or building ruins that are the result of destruction

cargo
Items brought on a journey aboard an airplane or ship

hazardous
Dangerous

microscopic particles
Pieces that are too small to be seen by the naked eye, and that require a microscope to be seen

mission
Specific task that a person or group is responsible for doing

olfactory
Connected or related to the sense of smell

paramedic
Person trained to help the injured before they are able to be brought to a hospital

SAR (Search and Rescue) Team
Dog handler and dog trained in search and rescue

SAR (Search and Rescue) Unit
Organization made up of dogs, handlers, and support personnel who go out on search and rescue missions

scurf
Microscopic particles constantly shed by all humans that carry the unique scent of the individual

shabrack
Coat or vest worn by a search and rescue dog that usually displays a cross or the word "rescue"

tracking
When a search and rescue dog sniffs the ground and low-growing plants to pick up a missing person's scent

for More Informatio

http://www.nasar.org/nasar/specialty_fields.php
Website of the National Association for Search and Rescue; includes the latest news and information on SAR dogs

http://dogs.about.com/cs/searchandrescue/
More information on various types of search and rescue dogs and missions

http://www.absarokasearchdogs.org
Website about canine SAR in Montana

http://www.sdsheriff.net/sar/aboutus/canine.html
Information on San Diego, California's canine search and rescue units

http://www.wemsi.org/bylaws.html
Shows the current bylaws from various search and rescue dog groups

Index